P9-DID-756

JAMES DASHNER

ALL ABOUT THE AUTHOR™

JAMES DASHNER

PHILIP WOLNY

ROSEN
PUBLISHING®

New York

Published in 2014 by The Rosen Publishing Group, Inc.
29 East 21st Street, New York, NY 10010

First Edition

Library of Congress Cataloging-in-Publication Data

Wolny, Philip.
James Dashner/Philip Wolny.—First edition.
    pages cm.—(All about the author)
Includes bibliographical references and index.
ISBN 978-1-4777-1763-9 (library binding)
1. Dashner, James, 1972–2. Authors, American—
20th century—Biography—Juvenile literature. I. Title.
PS3604.A83W86 2013
813'.6—dc23
[B]

2013010838

Manufactured in the United States of America

CPSIA Compliance Information: Batch #W14YA: For further information, contact Rosen Publishing, New York,
New York, at 1-800-237-9932.

CONTENTS

James Dashner could hardly believe it. He was in the middle of an author tour, hitting eight U.S. cities in three weeks, when he attended the BookExpo America (BEA) conference in May 2009.

Dashner rose early to attend BEA's annual Children's Author Breakfast. As a writer himself and a fan of other writers, he was excited to meet some of his peers—and some of his heroes, too. But he felt the most excited about seeing one particular writer: Judy Blume.

When it came to young adult (YA) fiction, Blume was a legend, beloved by fans from many generations. Dashner felt like a young musician seeing his favorite artist in person. He later wrote on his blog, "I wanted to say something, shake her hand, hug her, get down on my knees and thank her for providing all those books that—more than any other author by far—made me fall in love with reading as a kid. But I did nothing."

Luck was on Dashner's side, however. The star-struck young writer soon found himself in an elevator at the Random House offices with his hero. In a group of people that included

From humble beginnings, James Dashner has risen to become a beloved YA fiction author. His works include several multi-part series: *The Jimmy Fincher Saga*; *The 13th Reality*; and *The Maze Runner*.

Dashner's publicist, Blume, and Blume's publisher, he was introduced to his hero. Even better, Blume invited Dashner and a few others to have some tea and cupcakes.

After an hour with the friendly veteran YA author, Dashner still could hardly believe his luck. "You may laugh," he wrote later, "but it was as surreal as sitting down with Abraham Lincoln or Charles Dickens. Just amazing for me."

Things had come full circle for Dashner. He had read the work of Blume and other authors as a child and now was gaining dedicated fans for his growing list of YA fantasy novels. Just a few years earlier, he had been a writer struggling to make it while working full-time as an accountant. Since then, he had made the leap from aspiring writer to published author. Readers were now lining up for his autograph at book signings.

The hard work he put into writing his books has been a big factor in his success, but not the only one. Some of his biggest breaks have come from networking: taking the time and effort to meet other writers, booksellers, and readers to establish relationships and put his books into the hands of as many readers and publishing professionals as possible.

All the while, he has earned praise from readers and critics alike for his intricate plots and believable and sympathetic characters who are challenged by extraordinary situations in fantastical surroundings. Dashner appreciates his success all the more because he knows how much effort went into it. From humble beginnings as an office worker writing in his spare time, he has lived a life that many writers dream about but only some truly experience. Like each new revision, each step in the process has been a new adventure for James Dashner.

ONE

BECOMING AN AUTHOR

CHAPTER

J ames Smith Dashner was born in the small town of Austell, Georgia, about a half hour west of the state capital, Atlanta, on November 26, 1972, to John and Linda Dashner. They moved to nearby Duluth two years later. Unlike many writers, who always knew that they would make a career of writing stories and novels, Dashner blossomed later in life. He had an average, loving, all-American childhood with five siblings, and he was a big sports fan. Still, a creative spark shone through. As a boy, he would act out entire movies in the backyard with friends or family.

There were other signs that he had a literary and creative side. Like many children, the young Dashner loved books and reading. In middle school, he was inspired by the well-rounded characters that he found

Judy Blume, pictured here in 2012 at the *Los Angeles Times*' Festival of Books, in Los Angeles, California, was and remains one of Dashner's favorite all-time authors. Her honest and realistic coming-of-age stories have inspired many writers.

in books by Judy Blume, the popular YA author who wrote about the pains of growing up.

Dashner also lost himself in fantasy and science fiction. His early favorites included children's literature classics like C. S. Lewis's series *The Chronicles of Narnia* and Madeleine L'Engle's *A Wrinkle in Time*, as well as more mature books, like J. R. R. Tolkien's epic fantasies *The Hobbit* and *The Lord of the Rings* trilogy.

C. S. Lewis's book *The Lion, the Witch, and the Wardrobe* was the first installment in *The Chronicles of Narnia*, the immensely popular children's fantasy series that also inspired Dashner as a young reader.

The teenaged Dashner was a devoted fan of the futuristic science-fiction novel *Ender's Game*, by Orson Scott Card. His other favorite authors were thriller and horror writer Dean Koontz and horror writer Stephen King. King's novels, about regular people facing terrifying, fantastical situations, would greatly influence Dashner's own writing. Teenage mysteries such as the Hardy Boys also influenced him, as did adventure movie franchises like *Star Wars* and *Indiana Jones.*

Dashner wrote a bit during his youth. "I call the adolescent years the magic years of reading," he said in an interview with the *On and Beyond* blog in August 2012. "I wrote some short stories as a kid, and the biggest education I ever received came from reading." He has always thought of the teenage years, between the ages of twelve and seventeen, as helping form his imagination, especially when it came to fantasy fiction. He told the blog *Our Time in Juvie* in January 2012, "I think your brain when you're that young, there's a tiny part of it that believes it's real."

His childhood memories and reading experiences would resurface in his later work. At one point, someone had left an abandoned door in the woods near his home, and a young Dashner began imagining that something interesting was hidden beneath it. He later blogged, "*Narnia* was one of my

Another big inspiration for Dashner has been Orson Scott Card's novel *Ender's Game*. Card is shown here speaking at the Bookmarks Book Festival in Winston-Salem, North Carolina. Like Dashner, Card was raised in and remains part of the Mormon Church.

absolute favorite series growing up, so that contributed to my fantasy that something really cool was under that door."

DASHNER GOES TO COLLEGE (AND JAPAN)

Like one of his heroes, Orson Scott Card, Dashner has been a lifelong member of the Mormon Church, also known as the Church of Jesus Christ of Latter-day Saints (LDS). When he graduated from Duluth High School in Duluth, Georgia, in 1991, this upbringing was one major reason he decided to enroll at Brigham Young University (BYU) in Provo, Utah.

BYU is well known for having a student population that is almost entirely Mormon. While he would have doubts about his choice in the years to come, Dashner decided to seek a degree in accounting. Like many of his fellow students, he took a break early in his studies to fulfill a two-year volunteer commitment to be an LDS missionary overseas. Until that point, uprooting himself from his southern small town had been, in his own words, "about a huge a jump as I could possibly make in my life," as he related to the *Deseret News* in April 2010.

However, it was nothing compared to the change that he experienced when he ended up in Sapporo, Japan. "Actually, it was my LDS mission to Japan that was the bigger change. Coming out to Utah, you realize it's the same country, little bit different culture. Japan felt to me like a different world. I had this sense of wonder I've never forgotten," he told the *Salt Lake Tribune* in October 2011. During his assignment there, from 1992 to 1994, Dashner learned Japanese. His experience as a fish out of water also helped him describe the "otherworldly" experiences of his stories' characters later on.

This photograph is a nighttime view of the Japanese city of Sapporo, the capital of Hokkaido Prefecture. Dashner spent his two years as an LDS missionary based there, one of several Japanese cities with a Mormon mission.

DASHNER GROWS UP

Dashner came back to the United States from Japan and finished a combined bachelor of science in accounting (BSAcc) and a master of accountancy (MAcc) degree. Near the end of his studies, he married fellow BYU student and Utah native Lynette Anderson on February 14, 1998. He joked on his blog, "Yes, we got married on Valentine's Day. But that was only because I had a week off from school the next week, it was a Saturday, and neither of our moms would let us even consider getting married on Friday the 13th."

For the time being, it seemed that Dashner had it all: newly married with a promising, if uneventful, career working with numbers. Soon, however, the writing bug would bite him again.

A WRITER BLOOMS

James Dashner has paved his own road to success. His writing career started slowly and steadily built up steam. His rise was slightly unusual; he took a few unorthodox chances and steps initially. As with many writing success stories, it involved a combination of ability, hard work, luck, and a publisher willing to take a chance on an unknown talent.

EARLY BEGINNINGS: JIMMY FINCHER

Readers sometimes have a romantic, fantasy image of authors living glamorous, exciting lives after achieving overnight success. For a few, this may be true. However, for most writers, the reality is often far more modest. Some take years to sell a single story or manuscript, while others start small and build their way up. It can be a long, tough, and at times, lonely road.

Around 1998, as Dashner was finishing his accounting studies, he conceived of a child character named Jimmy Fincher, who encounters a magic door in the woods. At first, Dashner was not clear as to what that door was, nor how his protagonist and

DASHNER'S FIVE-YEAR PLAN

When he was just beginning his career in 2003, Dashner promised himself that he would become a full-time writer within five years' time. To truly keep this promise, "I told a bunch of my friends so I'd have witnesses and people to push me," he told *Writer's Digest* in 2010. It was a big commitment for a novice writer who was not only inexperienced in the business, but also had never actually met another author. This determination helped him stay strong while making such a profound change in his life while also working on limitations in his writing, taking constructive criticism, and avoiding the self-doubt and anxiety that many creative people experience. Dashner the accountant really saw himself as Dashner the writer.

the door would fit together in terms of the plot.

He reflected later on his blog, "[Fincher was] a dorky southern kid running around the woods with no clue that an evil door lay nearby, under which was something that would change the world forever. Problem: I didn't know what lay under the door, and I kept stalling with more and more of the ridiculous (not in a good way) antics of poor Jimmy Fincher."

A student strolls past the entrance to Brigham Young University (BYU) in Provo, Utah. With its student body almost entirely Mormon, it was one of the natural choices for James Dashner to complete his higher education.

Eventually, Dashner started over, this time doing a broad outline first. Between finishing school and starting a job, it took him a couple of years to get the story down on paper.

As a relative beginner, he later admitted, he wasn't nearly as good a writer then. He recalled on his blog in August 2007, "It wasn't very well written...and I still had a lot to learn. But I loved the story. I loved it with a passion, and I wanted others to read it." While part of his motivation for the story was to have something to read to his first child, Dashner realized that he had something special to share with a wider public.

By the middle of 2001, these ideas took form as Dashner's very first book, *A Door in the Woods*. In it, fourteen-year-old Jimmy Fincher witnesses a shocking event that leads to him becoming entangled in a quest away from home in Duluth, Georgia, not only across the country, but even into other worlds. He fights powerful, ancient forces in a battle to save reality itself.

Although some of the book's themes were dark, the young narrator is outspoken and funny, telling a suspenseful fantasy story filled with twists. Even while writing the first book in what would become the four volumes of the *Jimmy Fincher Saga*, Dashner knew the big surprise that would end the series.

SHOPPING AROUND

Dashner had a lot to learn—not only about writing but also about the publishing business itself. He first tried sending letters and manuscripts to some of the biggest publishing houses. He received rejection after rejection.

While he knew how slim his chances were, he was definitely disappointed. Though discouraged about making it as a writer, he didn't give up. Instead, he tried three small, regional companies. Cedar Fort, Covenant, and Deseret Book were publishers putting out books mainly for Mormon readers. Covenant and Deseret passed on Dashner's manuscript because their focus was not fantasy fiction.

His spirits rose when he opened a letter from Cedar Fort, based in Springville, Utah. Cedar Fort's acquisitions editor wrote him, saying that his eleven-year-old son had read the manuscript cover to cover and had loved the story. Soon, Dashner found himself on the phone with managing editor Chad Daybell, who seemed to like it, too.

AN UNUSUAL OFFER

Aspiring authors always hope for a lucky break. Usually, a publisher interested in a manuscript or idea agrees to pay an advance. When a publisher or other company asks for money up front from writers, it can be a warning sign that they are not honest or professional. Literary agents, who negotiate author contracts on their clients' behalf, will almost always consider this a terrible idea. Authors risk losing all their money to a company that they should not have trusted in the first place.

Even Dashner, an inexperienced first-time author who had no agent, was skeptical when Cedar Fort first pitched their idea. They explained that they wanted to publish *A Door in the Woods*, but they had never put out a YA fantasy book for a national market. It would be a risky investment, and they suggested he put up some of his own money to spread that risk around.

Under the deal's terms, Dashner would put up part of the publishing costs, and he was promised that money back if the book did well its first year in print. They would also agree to a contract for the whole series that he had planned out for Jimmy Fincher. Putting his fears aside, and trusting in the staff at Cedar Fort, the nervous author agreed to the deal. Years later, in an August 2007 blog post, he joked, "My agent, upon reviewing the contract three years later, said it will take her roughly a decade to forgive me for ever signing it."

A DOOR IN THE WOODS

Cedar Fort released *A Door in the Woods* in June 2003. Dashner thought the cover of the book could have been better, but he admitted that the cover artist had done the best she could for a book that was at first only published regionally. Small publishers often have limited funds to shop a book around, or market, to stores, reviewers, and readers. Dashner was nonetheless happy to have his book out there. National bookstore chains and independent bookstores carried it, even if there was little coverage.

He had mixed feelings about being published, especially since he had paid for part of it himself. "I felt like a bit of a fake," Dashner admitted in a later blog post. Even the first copies he received had the italics mysteriously taken out, a problem that thankfully was resolved quickly but had made him sick with anxiety.

ADVENTURES IN PUBLISHING

J ames Dashner had taken the first steps in following his dream of becoming a real author. Much work remained, however. Weak early sales did not help. Dashner went through many ups and downs, wondering if he had made a terrible mistake by signing the contract with Cedar Fort. Even though he saw that the publisher's staff was extremely supportive, he feared that almost no one would read his book.

POUNDING THE PAVEMENT

Initially, *A Door in the Woods* sold only a few hundred copies. Dashner believed in the story and knew it could do better. New to the literary world, he had not attended industry events until becoming an author.

But it was at a literary event that he was inspired to take matters into his own hands.

He attended an event where author Anita Stansfield spoke about her career. She was a successful romance writer and, like Dashner, was a member of the LDS church. Stansfield encouraged her audience to "pound the pavement" to increase awareness, and thus sales, of their books.

Dashner took her advice. He decided to put as much effort into personally marketing his book as he did into writing it. For the next two years, he threw himself into author signings. Many readers and publishing industry people have described him as kind, funny, and likeable. He used this charm when speaking to bookstore managers and employees, trying to put his work on the map.

He quickly learned the importance of getting his books into the hands of young readers more directly. Rather than just relying on bookstores, Dashner began visiting schools, too. Talking to whole classrooms of young readers soon began to pay off.

WORD OF MOUTH

All the charm in the world, along with good reviews, can only take a good book so far. Another important part in the commercial success of a book or any product is word of mouth. Readers who like a book tell their friends. Hopefully, those friends tell other

Anita Stansfield, a fellow author and Mormon, poses here on her front porch in Alpine, Utah, with some of her romance novels. Dashner was energized by Stansfield's advice to heavily promote his own books.

friends. Teachers, librarians, and bookstore staff may even have young people asking them for the book.

In the end, it was his growing audience that did much of Dashner's work for him. Word of mouth began to spread, and readers identified with and enjoyed Jimmy Fincher's exploits. Cedar Fort chipped in as well, working with an enthusiastic Dashner to set up events such as bookstore signings and school visits. They pounded the pavement along with Dashner, who was determined to prove himself. Eventually, the book sold thousands of copies, a great success for a small publishing house and a first-time author.

Dashner wrote about how impressed he was with the word-of-mouth phenomenon on his blog: "I still can't get over the coolness of this concept. People, at no obligation, are taking the time to encourage others to buy my book. That's like Christmas and Easter wrapped all into one."

CLIMBING THE LADDER OF SUCCESS, SLOWLY

Dashner had already written the second book in the *Jimmy Fincher Saga*, *A Gift of Ice*, before the first one even hit the shelves. With excitement spreading among readers, he continued work on the third installment, *The Tower of Air*. Dashner was still

THE AUTHOR AND THE ACCOUNTANT: A TALE OF TWO DASHNERS

For much of his writing career, James Dashner has had to balance his dreams of being an author with the daily reality of nine-to-five employment. While his rich and overactive imagination fueled the words that he put on paper in the evenings, lunch hours, and Saturdays, he felt stuck in his day job. He often described this as a split between the right, or creative, side of his brain, with the logical left side. For much of that time, he worked on budgeting for the LDS church. To develop new characters, plots, and other ideas, he often brainstormed while driving and especially in bed at night before going to sleep. He appreciated the discipline that his job gave him in meeting deadlines and organizing his work, but he hated accounting.

working a day job as a financial analyst, helping raise two young children, promoting the first book, and writing. He learned the value of networking. Meeting other authors and industry professionals, he asked for their advice and used these connections to arrange more book signings and other promotional events. This dedication would soon pay off in a big way.

Cedar Fort published *A Gift of Ice* in spring 2004. *The Tower of Air* followed only a few months after. From having no published work, Dashner now had three books on the market only a year after his first book came out.

JIMMY FINCHER GETS A MAKEOVER

Things got even better when Dashner got a call from Cedar Fort's Georgia Carpenter. The publisher wanted to release the fourth Jimmy Fincher book with a whole new look, including new cover art. He was more excited when they also decided to re-release the first three books to match the new look and even include inside illustrations. Cedar Fort asked him to help pick someone for the design makeover of the *Jimmy Fincher Saga*. He became nervous when one promising choice for the art-work pulled out at the last minute because of other commitments.

Dashner's bosses at his day job had recently transferred him to a new office nearby. It was in his first week that he told his new coworkers that he was an author and desperately needed a cover artist and illustrator. As he recounted on his blog, "They nonchalantly told me about a dude who worked the vending machines in the building [Michael Phipps].

Dashner signs a copy of his novel *The Death Cure*, part three of *The Maze Runner* series, at the Texas Book Festival in Austin, Texas. Dashner's new full-time job as a writer includes extensive travel to promote his work.

Apparently, this guy was really awesome with a little thing called art." Incredibly, he discovered this and caught the artist in time; it had been Phipps's last week on the job. Like Dashner, Phipps was a creative person stuck at a day job he disliked while waiting for a big break. He went on to do the covers and inside art for all four Jimmy Fincher books.

WAR OF THE BLACK CURTAIN

By 2005, Dashner had put the finishing touches on the conclusion of Jimmy Fincher's adventures. Cedar Fort released the fourth and final book, *War of the Black Curtain*, in August of that year and re-released the other books over the following year. With the new look, the books looked more appealing and professional.

NEW HORIZONS

Dashner was learning the ropes of the publishing industry and was growing as a writer. As much as he loved Jimmy Fincher and the world he inhabited, he was relieved and excited to move on to new projects.

One night in November 2005, he imagined teenagers trapped in a giant maze, finding their way while facing fearsome monsters. He pictured this story happening in a distant, dystopian future world in which the characters were subjected to experiments by an unseen force. Dashner rushed downstairs to write notes that would eventually become the basic story for *The Maze Runner*.

He wrote his new book in four months and finished the sixty-eight-thousand-word manuscript by March 2006. Excited by how much he liked the story, he began submitting it to agents. His former agent, Jenny Rappaport, liked it, but promised to get back to him. In July, she got back to Dashner, saying she would work to submit it to publishers but that it needed work.

Dashner again received rejection after rejection. Publishers liked the story but thought its characters and writing were not quite good enough. One publishing house, while rejecting it, thought the author had potential and liked his writing. For the time being, *The Maze Runner* had not found a home. Fortunately, that publishing company gave him another opportunity.

THE 13TH REALITY IS BORN

In late 2006, Dashner received a lunch invitation from Shadow Mountain Press. The publishing company had passed on *The Maze Runner* manuscript but had another idea: would he be willing to come up with a few other book proposals for it? Dashner jumped at the chance. He only had a week.

He went to work, brainstorming ideas for stories. As he wrote on his blog, "One idea was about a boy who finds out he's actually part of a virtual reality universe…It was basically *Pinocchio* meets *The Matrix*." Another was a story about aliens. He gave up on both when he revised an older idea of his that he really liked, a narrative about a young character receiving messages in the mail filled with riddles.

He hurried through three chapters and added a three-page synopsis of the rest of the story. It was initially called *The 19th Reality* and starred a child named Mason McGee. Dashner e-mailed his work ahead of his lunch meeting. On the big day, Chris Schoebinger and Lisa Magnum from Shadow Mountain told him that they wanted to do the book. The rest of the meeting saw Dashner riding high as they talked about ideas for a series of books based around the story.

GETTING TO WORK

Shadow Mountain hoped to release the first book of Dashner's new project in early 2008, but they needed the first draft much earlier: March 2007. It was already December 2006; Dashner would have to work fast. He wanted to get opinions from friends and family before turning it in, so he gave himself a personal deadline for the end of January. He forced himself to write at least one thousand words each day.

About a week before February, he had finished, with 88,639 words written. He was nervous about turning the book in. His publishers had only seen the earlier three chapters, and he crossed his fingers when giving it to them. He was relieved when they told him they loved the first draft.

Magnum, the book's editor, gave Dashner seven pages of notes. This made him nervous until he realized that there were mainly minor criticisms and queries. He went through a few rewrites.

Another lesson that Dashner was learning was not to get too attached to the details of a book if changing them would improve it. Magnum asked if he could come up with a catchier name for the main character than Mason McGee, something unique. The author later joked to blogger Kaleb Nation, "My publisher looked at me with a blank face and said it was awful (sorry to all you Mason McGees out there)." Dashner was disappointed at first. He blogged, "It really took awhile to reconcile that in my mind. Mason had become a part of me."

He decided to name his protagonist Atticus Higginbottom. The first name was actually the main character's name from an earlier manuscript that he had written and set aside, *The World Sifter*, and was inspired by a main characters in one of his childhood favorites, Harper Lee's classic *To Kill a*

Harper Lee, author of the American classic *To Kill a Mockingbird*, is photographed in a courthouse in 1961, a year after her book was published. One main character in her book, lawyer Atticus Finch, served as Dashner's inspiration in the creation of his protagonist Atticus "Tick" Higginbottom.

Mockingbird. Atticus Higginbottom, nicknamed "Tick," was born. Shadow Mountain's staff had accidentally started calling Dashner's story *The 13th*

Reality. Everyone had liked that better, and Dashner went along with their suggestion.

Dashner's newest series was becoming a reality. The fantasy tale about thirteen-year-old Tick Higginbottom, whose decisions in solving mysterious riddles would affect the survival of the world itself, was called *The Journal of Curious Letters*. Dashner had developed as a writer and was about to enjoy even greater success through a combination of luck and hard work. Shadow Mountain was bigger than Cedar Fort, with more resources for publishing and marketing.

THREE

CHAPTER

A NEW "DAY JOB": FULL-TIME WRITER

While writing professionally, Dashner spent years playing it safe by also working as an accountant. With a family to support in the early years, writing had not brought in enough money to pay the bills. But he wrote in his spare time, balancing job, family, and growing success as an author.

He had little choice because even the first two are more than full-time jobs for most people. Until he developed as a writer and sold more books, he would have to settle for finding the time he needed before and after work, even sneaking in some writing time during his lunch hour.

With his newfound success, Dashner realized that he had a chance to live every emerging writer's dream: to quit his "day job" and pursue writing full-time. "I don't

Every author who is fortunate to have the opportunity to abandon other work they only perform for a paycheck must carefully consider the benefits and drawbacks. It took Dashner a few years before he was able to live his dream.

want to keep working for five years and look back and think, 'If I would have devoted my full time to it, would I have been a best-selling author?'" Dashner told the *Salt Lake City Tribune* in March 2008.

WRITING AS A JOB

In August 2008, the time had finally come. Dashner gave notice to his employers that he would be leaving soon. Like any major life change, it was frightening but exhilarating. Now he could fill his days with the work that he really loved doing. He told the *Deseret News* in 2009, a year after going full-time, that he considered himself a "creative person trapped in an accountant's body, not the other way around."

Except for all the time he could now dedicate to his craft, everyday life did not change drastically for Dashner and his family. He told *Deseret News* that his recent success had let them "live comfortably." He observed that his wife, Lynette, remained levelheaded about the changes in their life. "I think she's still a little skeptical, to be honest…She's still making sure I don't go too wild buying extravagant things with my checks," he joked to the *News*.

REVISIONS: GETTING IT RIGHT

Few, if any, authors get a story right with the first draft. It may take two, three, or more drafts not only to get a book that the authors are satisfied with but also work that others will accept—and hence publish. This process can take a long time, even if others like the story and the book in general.

It can also be tedious and repetitive, and it is often Dashner's least favorite part of the process. One of the parts he hates most, he wrote on his

Revisions are part of the tough work of writing. There are few, if any, authors out there whose first version of a manuscript is the one that is eventually consumed by readers. Editors and readers, professional and otherwise, often provide vital feedback.

blog, was "deciding what to accept and to reject. Mainly because, by that point, I am sick to death of the book. Imagine reading the same book nine or ten times within the span of a few weeks." Since his very first book, Dashner has not only learned the value of revising on his own but also the importance of others' opinions of his writing. Among these have been the editors and agents who have helped him improve over time.

THE LONG JOURNEY OF
THE MAZE RUNNER

Constructive criticism can greatly improve a story. The story of how Dashner's original manuscript for *The Maze Runner* was kicked around the publishing world for a few years is one example. By 2007, he had set it aside to concentrate on *The 13th Reality*.

Almost two years later, he got a letter from Stacy Whitman of Mirrorstone Books, detailing how he could improve the story. "This letter was brilliant. She nailed everything that was wrong with it," Dashner blogged. He was excited because Mirrorstone said they would decide on whether to accept the book if Dashner rewrote the first fifty pages and included a synopsis. *The Maze Runner* was reborn as a book proposal.

He rewrote for a week straight. At first, he was shocked at how poor he thought his writing had been. The bright side, however, was that he had improved as a writer over the years. He rewrote much of the old material and added new elements.

The notes that Whitman provided were a huge help. One big change was giving the book's characters unique personalities, whereas earlier they seemed like slightly different versions of the same person. Another problem was how the beginning of the book dragged a bit. "The original version had this huge information dump near the beginning," Dashner blogged, a section that the author and others realized over-explained all the rules of the book's universe. Instead, he spread this information throughout the story, giving the narrative more mystery and surprises.

USING LANGUAGE

Another weakness that Dashner tackled was the language his characters used. Their dialogue sounded unrealistic for young people stuck in a parallel world. "Here these kids have been living in this other-world type place for years, and yet they spoke [like the] snotty-nosed brats at your local middle school," he said. Dashner fixed this by creating slang for the Gladers, the prisoners of the maze. It was a clever way to make his protagonists sound more realistic, while avoiding any harsh language that would kill the book's chances with young audiences.

THE HOME STRETCH

Both Dashner and Whitman were disappointed when Mirrorstone ultimately passed on The Maze Runner, even though a few of Whitman's colleagues liked it. Dashner soon met a new agent, Michael Bourret, through a fellow author. Bourret signed him as a client based on the revised story. He advised Dashner to fill out the entire backstory of the Maze

Runner universe, even if only some of it made it into the book.

All of this tinkering paid off. Bourret sent the *Maze* proposal to ten companies in May 2008. A month later, Dashner was having lunch with his mother, wife, and kids, when he got a call. Delacorte Press, an imprint of the international publisher Random House, wanted to publish *The Maze Runner*.

IN DEMAND

Dashner had entered the big leagues. Beginning at the small, regional Cedar Fort, he had worked his way up to Shadow Mountain and then up to Random House, the largest book publisher in the world. He was excited that more people might read *The Maze Runner* than all his previous books combined.

Delacorte senior editor Krista Marino described the excitement that Dashner's manuscript generated in her office. He had submitted eighty pages, plus an outline of the rest of the book. "After reading those finished pages, no one here wanted to read the rest of the proposal. We didn't want to know what happened before we saw the final manuscript," she told *Publishers Weekly* in October 2009.

JUGGLING PROJECTS

Dashner juggled spreadsheets and other projects at work before writing full-time. Now he was doing

Random House is a publishing subsidiary of the German media conglomerate Bertelsmann. The publisher, whose London, England, office is pictured here, signed Dashner to its Delacorte Press imprint in 2008, a move that signaled Dashner's entry into the publishing big leagues.

a job he loved but which required an equally delicate balance of his time. As he began *The Maze Runner*—also envisioned as a multipart series—he was still in the middle of *The 13th Reality*. The second book of that series, *The Hunt for Dark Infinity*, was due for release in May 2009, while book three, *The Blade of Shattered Hope*, was due in spring of 2010. Asked by the book blog *YA Highway* if juggling two series at once was hard, Dashner admitted that he had to work on each separately for a month or two at a time. "I can't work on both series at once or it gets way too confusing," he said.

On the other hand, he enjoyed mixing it up between the fantasy genre of *The 13th Reality* and the dark science fiction of the *Maze* series. The two series were very different, and many readers noticed that the latter was a bit more sophisticated than the former. Dashner agreed that the newer series, about young people stuck in a place, was also darker, with the characters encountering more troubling enemies and problems than he had previously written about.

However, he also underscored the book's theme of characters having to overcome obstacles in a positive way by working together. Despite its grimness, he differentiated it from the other YA books works that had inspired it, such as William Golding's *Lord of the Flies*. In Golding's youth adventure novel, a group of British boys turn on one another when they become castaways on a remote island in the Pacific Ocean. Dashner told *YA Highway*, "I think the most specific thing I did in building the community is that I wanted them to react differently from the kids in *LOTF*. Instead of degenerating into animals, I wanted them to become more organized, more lawful, more determined, never losing hope. I hope that's really how humans would react."

Throughout 2009, Dashner was busy at work. He turned in *The Maze Runner*'s sequel, *The Scorch Trials*, at the end of July. Almost immediately, he had to switch gears to finish *The Blade of Shattered*

Dashner holds his book *The Scorch Trials* at a bookstore event. The action-packed book is the second in *The Maze Runner* series, and picks up with sun flares having scorched Earth and a virus called the Flare also devastating the planet.

Hope. Meanwhile, paperback editions of the first two books of *The 13th Reality* series were scheduled for release during winter 2009–2010. It was an incredible first year of full-time writing, leaving Dashner equal parts excited and anxious about his prospects.

DASHNER HITS THE ROAD

With the publication of *The Maze Runner* in October 2009, Dashner now had the support of Delacorte's powerful marketing machine. Where he had once pounded the pavement to promote Jimmy Fincher in communities around Utah, he was now flying and driving all around the United States, with tours in 2009 for both Delacorte and Shadow Mountain. International readers were about to experience the book as well. Delacorte was pushing the book in Spain, Germany, and other markets.

It was exhausting and exciting. Dashner met dozens of authors and publishing pros, he connected with teachers and bookstore staff, and, most important, he engaged personally with a growing legion of fans. Readers and others he had only communicated with via social media were now becoming face-to-face acquaintances and even friends.

FACE-TO-FACE WITH FANS

Dashner enjoys meeting and talking with young readers in person, too. Even before *The Maze*

DASHNER'S SOCIAL NETWORK

In an increasingly wired world, James Dashner has used the Internet to engage closely with readers, and he has blogged regularly since 2005. It is now common for writers and other creative people to connect directly with their fans online on a regular basis; Dashner embraced these technologies early and often. His readers feel more connected and involved with his work because of this.

The reverse is also true—it is easier than ever for fans to connect to their heroes and create a community around a particular writer and his or her work. Dashner keeps his readers posted on new projects, future appearances, and even random thoughts on everyday life: what movie he just saw, his favorite books, and other opinions and observations. Besides his blog, Dashner also connects with his followers on social networking platforms like Facebook and Twitter.

Runner came out, he was overwhelmed by the positive response that he received on his travels. In a video interview with Random House Kids, he said, "I had the chance to go visit with some teenagers who had advanced copies. They grilled me for hours, asking what would happen in book two."

He had come a long way since his very first bookstore appearances, where he felt almost as if he had to beg store personnel and customers to check out his work. While his first book with Cedar Fort had a first-print run of only one thousand paperbacks, Shadow Mountain had printed forty thousand hardcover copies of *The Journal of Curious Letters* upon its release in 2008. A year later, *The Maze Runner*'s initial hardcover print run from Delacorte numbered one hundred thousand. There would be many runs to follow for all his books, including hardcover and paperback releases.

INSPIRATION AND CRAFT

F iction writers, like painters, designers, musicians, filmmakers, and other creative people, depend on many different things to do their work. Talent, dedication, and discipline are necessary ingredients for an author in his or her quest to tell a good story.

Writing for young readers may seem easy to some, but in fact it can be even more difficult. James Dashner has gained fans by creating fantastical worlds in which his heroes face important decisions with great consequences. Dashner's success also comes from doing so while making these worlds believable and by creating characters that his readers can identify with.

A writer's imagination is especially valuable in a genre like fantasy fiction. Dashner's inspiration comes from many

CHAPTER FOUR

sources. These include YA authors but also adult fiction in genres like fantasy, science fiction, and horror. Film, television, and even music inspire his writing, too. Perhaps most important, it is his own imagination, both as an adult and that of his inner child, that combines these influences to create his own, personal storytelling vision.

THE WORK OF OTHERS

Many writers and writing teachers agree that any good writer must read the work of others. This is recommended not only to discover and develop one's own writing style, but it also helps spark the imagination and improve a writer's work. Dashner would not be the author he is today without reading Judy Blume, Stephen King, Dean Koontz, Orson Scott Card, and many others. For example, he has compared his *Maze Runner* series to a loose combination of Card's *Ender's Game*, Golding's *Lord of the Flies*, and Louis Sachar's YA novel *Holes*. Aside from books, Dashner is a big fan of television and film, in particular the television show *Lost*, which incorporated fantasy and thriller themes.

A FERTILE IMAGINATION

Among Dashner's most helpful techniques has been simply setting aside time to think. Whether just daydreaming or intentionally brainstorming, it has

Stephen King is one of the most successful and prolific popular authors of all time and remains a huge inspiration for James Dashner and other current YA writers.

helped him come up with many of his ideas. One of the times when his imagination is most fertile is in his own bed, where he sometimes thinks for an hour or two before actually falling asleep.

Much of his inspiration comes while on the go— while driving. In addition to movies, he also loves film scores. Playing cinematic music in his car puts him into a creative mood. "Somehow that creates a movie atmosphere in my head and I can envision entire scenes while going down the freeway," he blogged in 2005.

FILM AS INSPIRATION

Dashner is a huge cinema fan and has developed as a writer in an era where many works of fiction, both newer and older, are

...haven't you, Gollum?

Movies are one of the sources that fuel Dashner's imagination. Here, live musicians accompany a showing of Peter Jackson's adaptation of J. R. R. Tolkien's *The Two Towers* at New York City's Radio City Music Hall.

finding a home onscreen. Many of his favorite childhood stories have been adapted into films that have become his favorites. He has told numerous journalists and bloggers that *The Lord of the Rings* is his favorite film series.

Films are especially important for his creative process, as Dashner told *Publishers Weekly* in August 2012. "I think cinematically," he said. "To me, the story unfolds like a movie, and then I try to convert that to the written word." Many of the situations readers encounter in *The Maze Runner* and *The 13th Reality* series make use of the suspense and plot twists viewers also encounter watching films.

THE WRITING PROCESS

Each writer has a way of working that works best for him or her, and Dashner is no exception. Some may figure out the entire basic plot of a story before writing a single word and have even the most minor details mapped out. Others have only a very general idea and discover along the way what will happen to their characters or how their plot should develop. While certain authors can write steadily for weeks and then only return to their manuscript at the end to make major revisions, others edit while writing. A writer may write very little per day or work nonstop every waking hour and put thousands of words on screen or on paper.

Dashner works in stops and starts. His output varies, sometimes depending on deadlines. Weeks may pass without him working, followed by nonstop writing for several months. He wrote the first draft of *The Journal of Curious Letters* in seven weeks. Without a specific deadline, he may think about a book for a long time before actually starting. All the while, he writes down ideas. He mostly works from a general outline that covers the main events in his plot. This outline is usually short—just one or two pages.

KNOWING HOW IT ENDS

Other writers figure out where their story is going along the way, but not Dashner. As he revealed in a December 2007 post on his blog, "It is very important to me to know how my book ends before I begin writing it. I know a lot of other authors don't do this. They say the characters whisk them away and decide the ending for them. That's great. For them." For him, however, knowing how the story ends does not limit his creativity or imagination.

Once he starts on whatever project he's working on, Dashner is absorbed in the story most of the time, even if he is doing something else. He never edits while writing. "I write the whole thing in one long burst of creativity, not worrying about how good or how cruddy the writing may be," he wrote

FAITH AND WRITING

Readers, journalists, and others occasionally ask Dashner if his Mormon faith influences his writing in any way. The author dismisses the connection, stressing in an interview with blogger Eric James Stone that his main goal "is to make my stories fun and exciting and full of surprises. I try to make my characters strong morally...But I don't have much interest in mixing religion with my writing." Moral lessons in his books are often indirect for both the characters and the readers. He told the *Salt Lake Tribune* in October 2011, "I love the concept of nothing being purely good or evil. I really wanted readers to question whether they could get desperate enough to do certain things."

on his blog. "Creativity and storytelling is all that matters that first go-around. Fix all the jive later."

A DAILY ROUTINE

His workday is often a mix of activities. When he's not traveling, he may blog, send and respond to e-mails, and review comments or feedback from his editors or other trusted readers. With a first draft of a manuscript to finish, he writes for a couple of hours first thing in the morning and will typically do another writing session in the afternoon. He will do three or four writing or edit-ing sessions daily. If he needs inspiration, he reads, watches a DVD, or goes to the movies to "juice up my creativity factory," as he described it on his blog, by experiencing storytelling in its various forms. "If I am having writer's block or I'm just not feeling it, I'll go see a movie in the middle of the day or I'll watch a couple of TV shows...It really gets me back into the creative mode."

RECURRING THEMES AND ELEMENTS IN DASHNER'S WORK

Even if writers do not explicitly plan them, certain themes and elements will appear in their work. Many of these may recur throughout a book, series, or even among different, unrelated works. Dashner's ultimate goal is to tell a good story, but certain themes and story elements are woven into many of his books.

Emily Ellsworth, in her review of *The Death Cure* for the *Deseret News* in October 2011, pointed out "the desperation and lengths to which a society will go to save itself...No one character in the story is truly good or evil." The choices that Dashner's char-acters make are often difficult, and he tries to make readers think about whether the end justifies the means in tough situations.

DASHNER'S ANTAGONISTS

Another element in Dashner's storylines is fearsome antagonists. *The Maze Runner*'s villains, including the half-animal, half-machine Grievers, and the powerful organization WICKED, which is revealed in its sequel, *The Scorch Trials*, create obstacles for the characters. Bloggers and journalists have commented on how such antagonists are compelling because adolescent readers identify with situations that they cannot control—for example, the way the maze's creators wipe all the inhabitants' memories. Their wins and losses against these enemies are especially interesting to teens.

At the same time, the difference between good and evil is never easy to figure out. *The 13th Reality*'s hero, Tick, encounters equally strange villains who are behind the mysterious letters containing riddles that he and his friends need to solve to save the realities. These powerful antagonists both help and create trouble for the characters as they discover their true natures throughout the series. Dashner throws the reader for a loop, however, because even villains, such as Mistress Jane, are sometimes shown sympathetically.

DYSTOPIA

As both a writer and a reader, Dashner has been attracted to dystopian fiction. His *Maze Runner* series is his best example of such fiction, in which characters live and struggle in a fictional world that is frightening or undesirable, the opposite of a utopia, or an ideal or perfect world or society.

In the August 2012 *Deseret News* review of *The Maze Runner* prequel, *The Kill Order*, Dashner explained how dystopian fiction could be scarier than books involving vampires or other supernatural elements. Such futures seem possible, especially when one follows today's news headlines: "I think this adds another layer of depth and interest...This could happen." Dashner believes that speculative fiction, which asks readers to ask the question "What if?," provides an exciting setting for good storytelling.

DASHNER'S CHARACTERS

With all the riddles and problems his characters are faced with, they are forced to be resourceful and creative. Blogger Kristine Wildner asked where his characters come from, and whether he identifies with them. He replied that he definitely sees himself in them. "I'm in their head, so they just naturally think like I do. The difference is I make them much,

Fantasy and science fiction books and film have exploded in popularity in recent years. Enthusiastic fans of Suzanne Collins's *Hunger Games* series line up for a midnight showing of the film adaptation of her book on March 22, 2012, in Hurst, Texas.

much braver!" he admitted. Tick from *The 13th Reality* is one of his favorite characters, Dashner revealed, because he is based on the author himself. He also relates to Thomas from *The Maze Runner*, but recognizes that he can only hope he could be as brave and capable in similar situations.

He takes issue with certain clichés in YA fiction and tries to avoid them when developing his heroes. He told blogger Kaleb Nation in February 2008, "I get so tired of the old standard—orphan kid who lives with people who hate him." While he admits that many children grow up in unhappy situations, he counters that he prefers to "write what you know," which is why he would rather write storylines about a situation familiar to him: a happy family with supportive parents.

LOOKING FORWARD

James Dashner has experienced even greater success recently, and he has felt blessed to try his hand at new storytelling formats, as well as see his work adapted in new ways. Like many authors, he realized that new technologies and media have changed the way that readers experience stories. As his readership grows in the United States and around the world, he is excited to try new things.

MAJOR MILESTONES

In September 2010, Dashner received news from his agent that he could not have dreamed of a few years earlier. *The Maze Runner* had hit the *New York Times'* Best Sellers list. In May 2012, he blogged that the book had spent more than one year in cumulative weeks on the list throughout several printings. Simply making it onto the list was an accomplishment that he attributed to his loyal readers. "I don't say this to brag, but to say how thankful I am to all of you for making it happen. I'm the happiest author on Earth!" he blogged.

ON A ROLL

In 2012, he kept writing and releasing work. *Maze Runner* fans had long anticipated a return to their favorite dystopian story line. *The Kill Order* was released on August 14, 2012, and was written as a prequel to the series and to explain the frightening world it portrayed. His characters face a world endangered by solar flares, starvation, floods, and other disasters.

That September, Dashner also released the fourth and final installment of *The 13th Reality*, *The Void of Mist and Thunder.* Fans had been waiting a long time, but he had been busy with other books. He blogged in May 2012, "I didn't want to do this book until I could do it right. Even if my readers had to wait, I know I owed it to them and that they would be glad I didn't rush it or do a shoddy job."

THE BIG SCREEN

In 2012, Dashner received more news that left the avid film fan nearly speechless: the film studio 20th

Even though James Dashner has gained a much larger fan base in recent years, book signings remain an important part of his job. Here, he signs copies of *The Kill Order* at a bookstore in Salt Lake City, Utah.

Century Fox had purchased the rights to make a movie based on *The Maze Runner* and perhaps even its sequels. Since he was so often inspired in his writing by movies, and even pictured their plotlines visually as one would with films, he was even more excited.

His agent had begun shopping around the idea to studios in 2009, but they both suspected that it took a while due to the state of the American economy and because film executives wanted to see how well his series did first. The time seemed ripe. The rights to Suzanne Collins's immensely popular trilogy *The Hunger Games* had recently been a hot item, and J. K. Rowling's Harry Potter series sold millions of books, its eight film adaptations earning hundreds of millions at the box office. It was a market and fan base that Dashner's unique storytelling powers could appeal to.

He had long dreamed about writing movies, too, and he has not ruled it out as a possibility. While many writers collaborate with screenwriters on scripts based on their original works, Dashner wasn't involved in his because the rights had been sold early on before he achieved wider fame, but also "because I think it's a skill I haven't developed yet," he told book blogger Kristine Wildner. He admitted to *Deseret News* in April 2010 that he often fantasized about being involved: "I wouldn't want to meddle with things. I'd just love to linger around the set and see what's going on."

As of early 2013, Fox had done a great deal of work on the script for *The Maze Runner* and was looking for a director. There was initial excitement when Catherine Hardwicke, the director of the film version of the YA vampire novel *Twilight*, was picked, but she dropped out. Instead, filmmaker Wes Ball, whose short animated film *Ruin* became a sensation and is soon to be adapted into a full-length movie, got the job. Fans were excited because *Ruin*'s post-apocalyptic theme promised to fit well with Dashner's own dystopian source material. Fox officially announced that *The Maze Runner* film's release date is February 14, 2014.

A CHANGING INDUSTRY

In addition to his stories' journey to the big screen, Dashner has risen in a transforming industry. Printed books are only one part of the experience for YA fiction fans nowadays. E-books have surged in popularity, and fans read them on their computers, tablets, and mobile devices. More companies, including educational publishers hoping to market their books as learning tools, are releasing stories and other content alongside multimedia tie-ins. These include interactive Web sites, games, social networks, study aids, and many other elements.

A MULTIPLATFORM EXPERIENCE

In December 2012, Dashner announced a whole new project on his Web site, the first of its kind that he had ever signed on for. Educational publisher Scholastic had selected him to help create a series of books, with accompanying multimedia to engage readers, called *The Infinity Ring.*

The story's premise centers on young characters going on time-travel adventures to fix a series of "Great Breaks" throughout history. Besides entertainment, the series aims to get readers excited about history, especially the causes and effects of important events. *The Infinity Ring* would tie into a Web site for readers, who could have their own time-travel adventures. With gaming one of the most popular hobbies, the series would have accompanying video games, plus a map tucked into the front covers of the books.

It was Dashner's chance to share in a collaboration similar to Scholastic's popular *39 Steps* franchise, a previous series of adventure novels. It would be a new challenge for him as a writer. He would also create the final installment and have to work extra hard to tie together the story's conclusion with the independent voices and ideas of his fellow authors.

Asked by *Publishers Weekly* in August 2012 if he was nervous about completing the series, he said he welcomed the opportunity. "That will be a big task," he said. "Until you write the last book...you always have a little bit of freedom to say, 'Well, that can get wrapped up later,' but I will have to tie up every loose end. It will be a challenge, but I'm excited." Dashner is particularly thrilled about incorporating his favorite historical figure, U.S. president Abraham Lincoln, into the plot.

Some critics have questioned if new technologies are distracting young people from actually reading, but Dashner holds a more optimistic view. His main goal is to entertain his readers while drawing in non-readers as well. He told *Publishers Weekly* that he hoped they would "feel a little bit more immersed in the story because of the video game and the maps that come with the books. Definitely one of our goals is to capture reluctant readers. I don't think anything's more rewarding than hearing you've helped someone gain a love of reading." Scholastic executive David Levithan agreed, telling the *Los Angeles Times* in August 2012, "It's a myth that kids are either readers or gamers. The truth is they're readers and gamers."

THE MORTALITY DOCTRINE

The worlds of gaming and cyberterrorism will be the backdrop for a new series from Dashner. In September 2012, Delacorte Press/Random House

CRITICS CLOSE TO HOME

Some of Dashner's most valuable critics have been his children and, most important, his wife, Lynette. She often provides him with feedback on manuscript drafts, reminding him of one rule many writers live by: show, don't tell. In one *Maze Runner* draft, he had a leader tell a newcomer to the Glade that he couldn't ask any questions. Lynette convinced him to allow the character to ask his questions but receive few answers, thus building the tension for readers. As his children mature, he hopes they can help him continue to connect with young readers, too. In October 2011, he told the *Salt Lake Tribune*, "My oldest is 11...Now that he and his friends are growing older, I'm going to have them read the manuscripts...I want to see if my voice is too 'old-mannish.'"

announced it would publish a new trilogy from him called *The Mortality Doctrine*. Book one of the series, *The Eye of Minds*, is scheduled for simultaneous print and e-book publication on October 8, 2013. According to Random House, the book follows the adventures of a gamer named Michael, who spends much of his time in a hyper-realistic online fantasy world called the VirNet. Michael's real and virtual worlds are turned upside down when the government asks him to capture a dangerous hacker holding VirNet users hostage.

COUNTING HIS BLESSINGS

Much has changed for Dashner in the decade since he came up with Jimmy Fincher's story, as an author, literary celebrity, and family man. He began writing around the time he married, and now he and Lynette have four children. With his newfound success, they were able to move to a new home to accommodate their growing family. They now live in South Jordan, a small city in the middle of Utah's Rocky Mountains, perfect for a family that loves the outdoors, including hiking and skiing.

Dashner is shown here with his fellow collaborators in *The Infinity Ring* series. In the front row *(from left)* are Lisa McMann, Carrie Ryan, and Jennifer A. Nielsen. In the back row *(from left)* are Matt de la Peña, Dashner, and Matthew J. Kirby.

He appreciates his success and tries to remain humble about it, often making light of it. He told blogger Steph Su in 2009 that his family loves what he does. "My kids brag at school about me. My five-year-old daughter likes to tell people she's famous. I'm trying to work on that," he joked.

GIVING BACK

Dashner often promotes the work of others on his blog, writing enthusiastically about works by known authors, acquaintances, or good friends he has made during his travels, and especially books he enjoyed by up-and-coming writers.

He expresses his gratitude at achieving his dreams by introducing his fans to such

Two people walk through a subdivision in South Jordan, Utah, the town that has become the home of the Dashner family. With its picturesque views and wilderness access, it proved an ideal area to relocate once Dashner grew more successful in his career.

writers on the good chance that they might enjoy them, too: "I feel like I just really appreciate what I'm finally starting to see and I really, really feel an obligation to help other writers because so many people have helped me and I know what they're going through."

DASHNER'S ADVICE TO WRITERS

Dashner often stresses how important it is to have a place to write down ideas. "Always have a notebook with you," he advises on his blog. "Jot down ideas, whenever, wherever. You will forget them even if you think you won't." It is advice he follows because one never knows when and where inspiration will strike.

Because of his humble beginnings, he also knows the uncertainty that writers face in getting their work finished and read. He admitted to blogger C. S. Bezas, "Rejection is part of the game. It hurts and it will always hurt." Dashner advises all writers to keep working and submitting their stories, and that through persistence their work will find a home. Few, if any, writers never suffer rejection, including literary superstars.

Many established writers and publishing professionals have helped Dashner climb the ladder. He blogged in April 2012, "Each step can be traced

Inspiration for characters, situations, plots, and other components of storytelling can strike anytime, which is why serious writers should always carry a journal, notebook, or other means of recording ideas with them, wherever they go.

back eventually to someone I met at a conference or something like that."

Along with determination, he also swears by writers' conferences and other events as valuable resources for writers that want to meet other writers, learn and improve their craft, and network to make connections. A writer never knows who may be a factor in his or her own big break: a bookstore employee, a publishing executive, a literary agent, or a fellow unpublished author.

He also stresses the obvious: ultimately, it is the story that counts the most and the writing that goes into it. He repeats the age-old advice that writers must actually write and do anything they can to improve their skills. The most surefire way is to write every day. Any beginning writer will see better results over time if he or she works hard. It was advice that James Dashner lived by and that has allowed him to live his dream.

ON JAMES DASHNER

Name: James Smith Dashner

Birth date: November 26, 1972

Birthplace: Austell, Georgia

Current residence: South Jordan, Utah

First publication: *A Door in the Woods*, Book One of the *Jimmy Fincher Saga*, published June 1, 2003, Cedar Fort Publishing, Springville, Utah

Marital status: Married

Spouse: Lynette Anderson Dashner

Children: 4

Siblings: 5

Education: B. B. Harris Elementary School; Duluth High School, Duluth, Georgia, 1991; Brigham Young University, Provo, Utah, 1999, master of accountancy

Former occupation: Certified public accountant (CPA)/financial analyst

Writing genre: Young adult fantasy and science fiction

Hobbies: Reading, hiking, skiing, watching movies, and traveling

Major awards: Whitney Award for Best Youth Fiction (2008) for *The Journal of Curious Letters*; Children's Librarians of New Hampshire (CHILIS) Isinglass Teen Read Award (2011) for *The Maze Runner*; Georgia Peach Book Awards for Teen Readers (2011–2012)

for *The Maze Runner*; Kentucky Reading
Association's Kentucky Bluegrass Award for
Grades 9–12 (2011) for *The Maze Runner*; Missouri
Association of School Librarians' Truman Readers
Award (2012) for *The Maze Runner*; New York State
Reading Association Charlotte Award (2012) for
The Maze Runner; Oregon Reader's Choice Award,
Senior Division (2011–2012) for *The Maze Runner*.

ON JAMES DASHNER'S WORK

The Jimmy Fincher Saga

A walk in the woods hurls young Jimmy Fincher into an adventure where reality is not what it seems. Fincher must deal with powerful forces as he receives The Four Gifts that will help him fight an ancient conspiracy, traveling all over the world in a race against time to save the world.

A Door in the Woods: June 1, 2003, Cedar Fort

A Gift of Ice: February 1, 2004, Cedar Fort

The Tower of Air: July 1, 2004, Cedar Fort

War of the Black Curtain: August 1, 2005, Cedar Fort

The 13th Reality

Thirteen-year-old Atticus "Tick" Higginbottom receives a strange letter in the mail and soon must decipher clues to solve twelve riddles that unlock the doors to alternate realities. Tick enlists the help of other letter recipients like him to prevent the destruction of the realities by powerful and mysterious enemies.

The Journal of Curious Letters: March 8, 2008, Shadow Mountain

The Hunt for Dark Infinity: March 4, 2009, Shadow Mountain

The Blade of Shattered Hope: April 7, 2010, Shadow Mountain

The Void of Mist and Thunder: September 11, 2012, Shadow Mountain

The Maze Runner

A group of adolescents, their memories wiped by a powerful, unseen force, find themselves in the Glade, a world at the heart of a forbidding maze. Thomas, a new arrival, joins forces with his fellow Gladers to unlock the secret of their imprisonment.

The Maze Runner: October 6, 2009, Delacorte Press/Random House

The Scorch Trials: October 12, 2010, Delacorte Press/Random House

The Death Cure: October 11, 2011, Delacorte Press/Random House

The Kill Order (Prequel): August 14, 2012, Delacorte Press/Random House

(The film company 20th Century Fox purchased the movie rights to the book *The Maze Runner*, with a release date in 2014.)

The Infinity Ring

Time-traveling youngsters embark on adventures in order to fix a series of breaks within the fabric of history itself.

Infinity Book 1: A Mutiny in Time: August 28, 2012, Scholastic, Inc.

The Maze Runner (2009)

"Dashner knows how to spin a tale and make the unbelievable realistic. Hard to put down, this is clearly just a first installment, and it will leave readers dying to find out what comes next."
—*Kirkus Reviews*, September 15, 2009

"*The Maze Runner* by James Dashner is an action-packed novel that will leave readers thrilled to read the other installments in the series."
—Rebecca Danielle, *Seattle Post-Intelligencer*, November 15, 2012

The Scorch Trials (2010)

"Taut and bleak, continually intriguing and surprising, this [*The Scorch Trials*] is a solid sequel that keeps both Thomas and readers wondering what is really going on."—*Kirkus Reviews*, October 1, 2010

The Death Cure (2011)

"'The Death Cure' will not disappoint as the action-packed conclusion to 'The Maze Runner' series. Filled with plot twists and James Dashner's explosive action scenes, forget putting this book down until the very end."—Emily Ellsworth, *Deseret News*, October 8, 2011

The Kill Order (2012)

"Dashner has crafted a clever prequel [*The Kill Order*] that will appeal to fans anxious to see where *The Maze Runner* came from, while enticing those unfamiliar with the later books." — *Publishers Weekly*, August 20, 2012

The Journal of Curious Letters (2008)

"I found *The Journal of Curious Letters* to be both creative and fun...In all, I had a wonderful time reading this book and would recommend it to most fantasy readers ages 12 and up." — J. Mitchell, *YA Book Central*, March 2, 2009

"This new young adult fantasy by bestselling author James Dashner is riveting, entertaining and scary, all at the same time." — Tristi Pinkston, Families.com, March 5, 2008

A Mutiny in Time (2012)

"*A Mutiny in Time* features tight plotting, snappy dialogue, and a judicious balance of humor and suspense. The story moves at a breathless pace." — Rick Riordan, *New York Times Book Review*, August 23, 2012

1972 James Smith Dashner is born on November 26, in Austell, Georgia.

1974 The Dashners move to nearby Duluth, Georgia.

1991 Dashner graduates from Duluth High School; he enrolls at Brigham Young University (BYU) to study accounting.

1992–1994 He volunteers as a missionary for the Latter-Day Saints (Mormon) mission in Sapporo, Japan.

1998 Dashner marries fellow BYU student and Utah native Lynette Anderson on February 14, Valentine's Day; he conceives of his first fictional character, Jimmy Fincher.

2001 He finishes the first draft of *A Door in the Woods*; he begins submitting the manuscript to potential publishers.

2003 Cedar Fort publishes *A Door in the Woods*, with financial help from Dashner himself.

2004 Cedar Fort publishes Books 2 and 3 of the *Jimmy Fincher Saga*: *A Gift of Ice* and *The Tower of Air*.

2005 *War of the Black Curtain*, Book 4 of the *Jimmy Finger Saga*, is released; Dashner develops the idea for *The Maze Runner*.

2006 Dashner begins submitting *The Maze Runner* to publishers; Shadow Mountain signs him to create *The 13th Reality* series.

2008 Shadow Mountain publishes *The Journal of Curious Letters*, Book 1 of *The 13th Reality*; Delacorte Press agrees to publish *The Maze Runner*.

2009 Kirkus Reviews selects *The Maze Runner* as one of the best young adult books of the year; Shadow Mountain publishes *The Hunt for Dark Infinity*, the second book of *The 13th Reality*.

2010 Delacorte Press releases the sequel to *The Maze Runner*, *The Scorch Trials*; *The Maze Runner* makes it on to the best-seller list of the *New York Times*.

2011 *The Death Cure*, Book 3 of *The Maze Runner* series, is released.

2012 The fourth and final installment of *The 13th Reality* series, *The Void of Mist and Thunder*, is published by Shadow Mountain; Delacorte Press releases the prequel to *The Maze Runner* series, *The Kill Order*; film studio 20th Century Fox picks up the rights to produce a movie based on *The Maze Runner*; Scholastic publishes his *A Mutiny in Time*, the first installment of its new book series and multimedia learning platform.

2013 20th Century Fox officially announces the release date of the first film in *The Maze Runner* trilogy as February 14, 2014; Delacorte Press/Random House announces October 8, 2013, as the release date for the print and e-book versions of *The Eye of Minds*, Dashner's first installment in a planned trilogy about cyberterrorism and virtual reality called *The Mortality Doctrine*.

ACQUISITIONS EDITOR An editor at a publishing company in charge of seeking new books and writing talent.

ANTAGONIST The character in a story that opposes, or comes into conflict with, the protagonist.

CUMULATIVE Increasing by successive additions; for example, the total amount of rainfall somewhere in a particular year.

DRAFT An early version of a final work.

DYSTOPIAN Refers to fictional works that portray imaginary worlds or societies that are frightening or undesirable to live in.

FRANCHISE Refers to works that belong to a particular series of books, films, or other media properties.

LDS The abbreviation for the Church of Latter-day Saints, also known as the Mormon Church.

LEGION A very large or vast group of people.

LITERARY AGENT A paid representative of an author who represents the client's financial interests when dealing with publishing companies and other entities.

NETWORKING The process of meeting people to create mutually beneficial economic relationships.

POST-APOCALYPTIC Describes a fictional setting in which the characters must deal with the after-effects of a terrible event, such as a nuclear war or other disaster.

POUND THE PAVEMENT An idiom that means to aggressively execute a task—generally, to look for a job, seek financial support, or spread a message.

PRINT RUN The amount of copies of a book produced at any one time.

PROTAGONIST The hero or heroine, or main character, of a story.

PUBLICITY Awareness that is generated for a book or to help popularize it among readers and the media; also part of the staff of a publishing company charged with that task.

REVISION An unfinished copy of a manuscript or other written work, upon which changes are still being made.

SPECULATIVE FICTION Fiction that incorporates supernatural, fantastical, or science-fiction elements.

SYNOPSIS A brief summary of a larger or longer work, such as a novel.

UNORTHODOX Unusual, untraditional, or typically unaccepted.

YA Abbreviation for young adult, referring to fiction or nonfiction writing.

FOR MORE INFORMATION

Canadian Authors Association
74 Mississaga Street East
Orillia, ON L3V 1V5
Canada
Web site: http://www.canauthors.org
The Canadian Authors Association promotes the literary
community throughout Canada.

Cedar Fort Publishing and Media
2373 W. 700 South
Springville, UT 84663
(801) 489-4084
Web site: http://www.cedarfortbooks.com
Cedar Fort is a Utah-based, regional publisher of life-
style, inspirational, and fiction books, which
published James Dashner's first series, *The
Jimmy Fincher Saga*.

Delacorte Press/Random House
1745 Broadway
New York, NY 10019
(212) 782-9000
Web site: http://www.randomhouse.com
Random House is an international publisher of general-
interest trade books. Its subsidiary and imprint
Delacorte Press is the home of *The Maze Runner*
series.

EDGE Science Fiction and Fantasy Publishing/
Tesseract Books
P.O. Box 1714

Calgary, AB T2P 2L7
Canada
(403) 254-0160
Web site: http://www.edgewebsite.com
EDGE/Tesseract is a publisher of science-fiction and
    fantasy anthologies.

James Dashner's Official Web Site
Web Site: http://www.jamesdashner.com
Dashner's Web site includes a brief biography,
    upcoming events, Dashner's blog, and informa-
    tion about his published works.

Science Fiction & Fantasy Writers of America (SFWA)
P.O. Box 3238
Enfield, CT 06083-3238
Web site: http://www.sfwa.org
The SFWA is a professional organization for authors
    of science fiction, fantasy, and related genres.

Shadow Mountain Publishing
P.O. Box 30178
Salt Lake City, UT 84130-0178
Web site: http://www.shadowmountain.com
Shadow Mountain is the publisher of James
    Dashner's *13th Reality* series and publishes
    children's fantasy, picture books, adult inspira-
    tion, history, and business titles.

Society of Children's Book Writers and Illustrators (SCBWI)
8271 Beverly Boulevard

Los Angeles, CA 90048
(323) 782-1010
Web site: http://www.scbwi.org
The SCBWI is an international professional organization
    for writers and illustrators of children's literature
    founded in 1971.

Teen Ink
Box 30
Newton, MA 02461
(617) 964-6800
Web site: http://www.teenink.com
Teen Ink is a U.S. teen magazine focused on writing
    and art by teens, ages thirteen to nineteen.

U.S. Copyright Office
101 Independence Avenue SE
Washington, DC 20559-6000
(202)707-3000 or (877)476-0778
Web site: http://www.copyright.gov
This government site is a must for writers of any age. It
    provides detailed information about copyright and
    even a section for registering your written work.

Writer's Digest
10151 Carver Road, Suite 200
Cincinnati, OH 45242
(715) 445-4612
Web site: http://www.writersdigest.com
Writer's Digest is a publisher of resources for profes-
    sional writers and publishes the annual *Writer's*

Market reference book for authors to connect with agents and publishers.

Young Adult Library Services Association (YALSA)
50 East Huron Street
Chicago, IL 60611
(800) 545-2433
Web site: http://www.ala.org/yalsa
YALSA is a division of the American Library Association
    (ALA) that advocates for teen-oriented literary issues.

WEB SITES

Due to the changing nature of Internet links, Rosen Publishing has developed an online list of Web sites related to the subject of this book. This site is updated regularly. Please use this link to access the list:

http://www.rosenlinks.com/AAA/dash

Albert, Lisa Rondinelli. *Lois Lowry: The Giver of Stories and Memories* (Authors Teens Love). Berkeley Heights, NJ: Enslow Publishers, 2007.

Bankston, John. *Christopher Paolini* (Who Wrote That?). New York, NY: Chelsea House Publishing, 2010.

Benke, Karen. *Rip the Page!: Adventures in Creative Writing.* Boston, MA: Roost Books, 2010.

Brown, Tracy. *Stephanie Meyer* (All About the Author). New York, NY: Rosen Publishing, 2013.

Collins, David R. *J. R. R. Tolkien* (Just the Facts Biographies). Minneapolis, MN: Lerner Classroom Books, 2005.

Faktarovich, Anna. *Interviews with Best-Selling Young Adult Writers: Pennsylvania Literary Journal.* Tucson, AZ: Anaphora Literary Press, 2013.

Greene, Meg. *Louis Sachar* (Library of Author Biographies). New York, NY: Rosen Publishing, 2003.

Grundell, Sara. *Fame: Suzanne Collins.* Beverly Hills, CA: Bluewater Productions, 2012.

Hoover, Elizabeth. *Suzanne Collins* (People in the News). Farmington Hills, MI: Lucent Books, 2012.

Kenneally, Miranda. *Dear Teen Me: Authors Write Letters to Their Teen Selves* (True Stories). San Francisco, CA: Zest Books, 2012.

Krohn, Katherine. *Stephenie Meyer: Dreaming of Twilight* (USA Today Lifeline Biographies). Minneapolis, MN: Twenty-First Century Books, 2010.

Le Guin, Ursula K. *The Wild Girls* (Outspoken Authors). Oakland, CA: PM Press, 2011.

Lynch, Doris. *J. R. R. Tolkien: Creator of Languages and Legends* (Great Life Stories). New York, NY: Franklin Watts/Scholastic, 2003.

Marcus, Leonard S., ed. *The Wand in the Word: Conversations with Writers of Fantasy.* Somerville, MA: Candlewick Press, 2006.

McCormick, Lisa Wade. *Christopher Paolini* (All About the Author). New York, NY: Rosen Publishing, 2013.

Moonshower, Candie. *Vivian Vande Velde: Author of Fantasy Fiction* (Authors Teens Love). Berkeley Heights, NJ: Enslow Publishers, 2009.

Owen, James A. *Secrets of the Dragon Riders: Your Favorite Authors on Christopher Paolini's Inheritance Cycle; Completely Unauthorized.* Dallas, TX: Smart Pop, 2012.

Piddock, Charles. *Ray Bradbury: Legendary Fantasy Writer* (Life Portraits). Milwaukee, WI: Gareth Stevens Publishing, 2009.

Potter, Ellen, Anna Mazer, and Matt Phelan. *Spilling Ink: A Young Writer's Handbook.* New York, NY: Square Fish Publishing, 2010.

Reichard, Susan E. *Philip Pullman: Master of Fantasy* (Authors Teens Love). Berkeley Heights, NJ: Enslow Publishers, 2006.

Saxena, Shalini. *Anthony Horowitz* (All About the Author). New York, NY: Rosen Publishing, 2012.

Sexton, Colleen. *J. K. Rowling* (Biography). Minneapolis, MN: First Avenue Editions, 2012.

Wheeler, Jill C. *Suzanne Collins* (Children's Authors). Edina, MN: Checkerboard Library, 2013.

Willett, Edward. *Orson Scott Card: Architect of Alternate Worlds* (Authors Teens Love). Berkeley Heights, NJ: Enslow Publishers, 2006.

Wynne Jones, Diana. *Reflections: On the Magic of Writing.* New York, NY: Greenwillow Books, 2012.

Abrams, Rachel. "Catherine Hardwicke in Talks to Run 'Maze.'" *Variety*, December 2, 2010. Retrieved December 19, 2012 (http://www.variety.com/article/VR1118028298).

Andrew, Victoria. "Book Review for 'A Mutiny in Time' by James Dashner." *West Orlando News*, June 14, 2012. Retrieved December 20, 2012 (http://westorlandonews.com/2012/06/14/book-review-for-a-mutiny-in-time-by-james-dashner).

Bezas, C. S. "Interview with James Dashner, LDS Author." Bella Online. Retrieved December 20, 2012 (http://www.bellaonline.com/articles/art55919.asp).

Billington, Alex. "'Ruin' Director Wes Ball Lands 'The Maze Runner' Directing Gig at Fox." FirstShowing .net, August 24, 2012. Retrieved January 27, 2013 (http://www.firstshowing.net/2012/ruin -director-wes-ball-lands-the-maze-runner -directing-gig-at-fox).

Bolle, Sonja. "Word Play: Murky, Paranoid Worlds Fit for the Teen Reader." *Los Angeles Times*, February 14, 2010. Retrieved January 20, 2013 (http://www.latimes.com/entertainment/news/la-caw -word-play14-2010feb14,0,2696275.story).

Book Adventures. "James Dashner Lecture." June 19, 2011. Retrieved January 10, 2013 (http://dianasamazingbookadventures.blogspot .com/2011/06/james-dashner-lecture.html).

Carpenter, Susan. "Scholastic's 'Infinity Ring' a Multimedia Ride Through History." *Los Angeles*

Times, August 26, 2012. Retrieved January 27, 2013 (http://articles.latimes.com/2012/aug/26/entertainment/la-ca-kids-middle-grade-infinity-ring-feature-20120826).

Chin, Chester. "There's a Little Kid in Author James Dashner." *The Star*, September 23, 2012. Retrieved December 1, 2012 (http://thestar.com.my/lifestyle/story.asp?file=/2012/9/23/lifebookshelf/12045531&sec=lifebookshelf).

CosmoGirl. "Meet the *Maze Runner* Author, James Dashner." *Seventeen*, January 20, 2011. Retrieved December 14, 2012 (http://www.seventeen.com/cosmogirl/james-dashner-maze-runner-interview).

Danielle, Rebecca. "Book Review: *The Maze Runner* by James Dashner." *Seattle Post-Intelligencer*, November 15, 2012. Retrieved January 2, 2013 (http://www.seattlepi.com/lifestyle/blogcritics/article/Book-Review-The-Maze-Runner-by-James-Dashner-4042300.php).

Dashner, James. "About James." JamesDashner.com, 2012. Retrieved December 1, 2012 (http://www.jamesdashner.com/about).

Dashner, James. "Are You There, Judy? It's Me, James." JamesDashner.blogspot.com, October 27, 2009. Retrieved December 15, 2012 (http://jamesdashner.blogspot.com/2009/10/are-you-there-judy-its-me-james.html).

Dashner, James. "Behind the Book: The Magic of Discovery." Bookpage.com, August 14, 2012. Retrieved December 20, 2012 (http://

bookpage.com/behind-the-book/behind
-the-book%3A-the-magic-of-discovery).

Dashner, James. "Best Decade of My Life."
JamesDashner.com, February 13, 2008. Retrieved
January 15, 2013 (http://www.jamesdashner.com/
best-decade-of-my-life).

Dashner, James. "BookExpo America Day 4."
JamesDashner.com, June 2, 2008. Retrieved
January 7, 2013 (http://www.jamesdashner.com/
book-expo-america-day-4).

Dashner, James. "Change the World Tour: Day 4."
JamesDashner.com, March 6, 2008. Retrieved
January 20, 2013 (http://www.jamesdashner.com/
change-the-world-tour-day-4).

Dashner, James. "Dave Wolverton—Dystopia."
JamesDashner.com, November 7, 2011. Retrieved
January 12, 2013 (http://www.jamesdashner.com/
dave-wolverton-dystopia).

Dashner, James. "Eight Random Things." JamesDashner
.com, October 9, 2007. Retrieved December 20,
2012 (http://www.jamesdashner.com/eight
-random-things).

Dashner, James. "A Few Quick Things." JamesDashner.
com, March 26, 2008. Retrieved January 11, 2013
(http://www.jamesdashner.com/a-few-quick-things).

Dashner, James. "First Day on the Job: Michael Phelps;
Jason Lezak." JamesDashner.com, August 11,
2008. Retrieved January 20, 2013 (http://www
.jamesdashner.com/first-day-on-the-job-michael
-phelps-jason-lezak).

Dashner, James. "5 Years of Being an Author." JamesDashner.com, June 25, 2008. Retrieved December 14, 2012 (http://www.jamesdashner .com/5-years-of-being-an-author).

Dashner, James. "Further Thoughts." JamesDashner .blogspot.com, August 26, 2005. Retrieved December 20, 2012 (http://www.jamesdashner.com /further-thoughts).

Dashner, James. "Great News from Borders Bookstores." JamesDashner.blogspot.com, February 27, 2008. Retrieved December 20, 2012 (http://jamesdashner .blogspot.com/2008/02/great-news-from-borders -bookstores.html).

Dashner, James. "Hmm, What to Talk About." JamesDashner.com, December 13, 2007. Retrieved December 1, 2012 (http://www.jamesdashner.com/ hmm-what-to-talk-about).

Dashner, James. "How I Got Here, Part 1: The Birth of Jimmy Fincher." JamesDashner.com, August 28, 2007. Retrieved December 1, 2012 (http://www .jamesdashner.com/how-i-got-here-part1 -the-birth-of-jimmy-fincher).

Dashner, James. "How I Got Here, Part 2: My First Book." JamesDashner.com, August 29, 2007. Retrieved December 1, 2012 (http://www.jamesdashner.com/ how-i-got-here-part-2-my-first-book).

Dashner, James. "How I Got Here, Part 3: Pounding the Pavement." JamesDashner.com, August 31, 2007. Retrieved December 1, 2012 (http://www .jamesdashner.com/how-i-got-here-part-3 -pounding-the-pavement).

Dashner, James. "How I Got Here, Part 4: Michael Phipps." JamesDashner.com, September 4, 2007. Retrieved December 1, 2012 (http://www.jamesdashner.com/how-i-got-here-part-4-michael-phipps).

Dashner, James. "How I Got Here, Part 5: The Three Amigos." JamesDashner.blogspot.com, September 11, 2007. Retrieved December 1, 2012 (http://jamesdashner.blogspot.com/2007/09/how-i-got-here-part-5-three-amigos.html).

Dashner, James. "How I Got Here, Part 6: *The 13th Reality*." JamesDashner.blogspot.com, September 14, 2007. Retrieved December 1, 2012 (http://jamesdashner.blogspot.com/2007/09/how-i-got-here-part-6-13th-reality.html).

Dashner, James. "How I Got Here, Part 7: Shadow Mountain." JamesDashner.blogspot.com, September 19, 2007. Retrieved December 1, 2012 (http://jamesdashner.blogspot.com/2007/09/how-i-got-here-part-7-shadow-mountain.html).

Dashner, James. "How I Got Here, Part 8: To the Present Day." JamesDashner.blogspot.com, October 1, 2007. Retrieved December 1, 2012 (http://jamesdashner.blogspot.com/2007/10/how-i-got-here-part-8-to-present-day.html).

Dashner, James. *The Journal of Curious Letters.* Salt Lake City, UT: Shadow Mountain, 2008.

Dashner, James. *The Kill Order.* New York, NY: Scholastic, 2012.

Dashner, James. *The Maze Runner.* New York, NY: Delacorte Press, 2009.

Dashner, James. "One Year Anniversary—MAZE Giveaway." JamesDashner.com, August 10, 2009. Retrieved December 14, 2012 (http://www.jamesdashner.com/one-year-anniversary-maze-giveaway).

Dashner, James. "Q&A: Aspiring Writers." JamesDashner.com, October 23, 2007. Retrieved January 10, 2013 (http://www.jamesdashner.com/qa-aspiring-writers).

Dashner, James. "Q&A: Get Out of Stuckland." JamesDashner.com, May 14, 2008. Retrieved January 10, 2013 (http://www.jamesdashner.com/qa-get-out-of-stuckland).

Dashner, James. "Q&A: Publicity." JamesDashner.blogspot.com, September 7, 2007. Retrieved December 1, 2012 (http://jamesdashner.blogspot.com/2007/09/q-publicity.html).

Dashner, James. "Q&A: What to Do After the Book Is Written." JamesDashner.com, December 27, 2007. Retrieved January 10, 2013 (http://www.jamesdashner.com/qa-what-to-do-after-the-book-is-written).

Dashner, James. "Q&A 2012: Part 2." JamesDashner.com, April 18, 2012. Retrieved January 10, 2013 (http://www.jamesdashner.com/qa-2012-part-2).

Dashner, James. "Question of the Day." JamesDashner.com, August 23, 2005. Retrieved December 30, 2012 (http://www.jamesdashner.com/question-of-the-day-3).

Dashner, James. *The Scorch Trials.* New York, NY: Delacorte Press, 2010.

Dashner, James. "The Tale of *The Maze Runner*." JamesDashner.blogspot.com, July 16, 2008. Retrieved December 1, 2012 (http://jamesdashner .blogspot.com/2008/07/tale-of-maze-runner.html).

Dashner, James. "*The 13th Reality*, Book 4." JamesDashner.com, May 24, 2012. Retrieved January 15, 2013 (http://www.jamesdashner.com/ the-13th-reality-book-4).

Dashner, James. "Three Days…and a Story." JamesDashner.blogspot.com, April 25, 2011. Retrieved December 14, 2012 (http://jamesdashner .blogspot.com/2011/04/three-days.html).

Dashner, James. "The Wednesday List." JamesDashner .com, June 17, 2009. Retrieved December 15, 2012 (http://www.jamesdashner.com/the-wednesday-list).

Ellsworth, Emily. "Book Review: 'The Death Cure' Is an Action-Packed Conclusion to the '*The Maze Runner*' Series." *Deseret News*, October 8, 2011. Retrieved January 11, 2013 (http://www .deseretnews.com/article/705392088/Book -review-The-Death-Cure-is-an-action-packed -conclusion-to-The-Maze-Runner-series .html?pg=all).

Fulton, Ben. "James Dashner: Writing Through the 'Maze Runner.'" *Salt Lake Tribune*, October 5, 2011. Retrieved December 10, 2012 (http://www.sltrib .com/sltrib/entertainment/52648767-81/books -maze-dashner-readers.html.csp).

Haddock, Sharon. "'The Kill Order' Explains Much of the Series' Story." *Deseret News*, August 11, 2012. Retrieved January 4, 2013 (http://www

.deseretnews.com/article/865560474/The-Kill
-Order-explains-much-of-the-series-story
.html?pg=all).

Haraldsen, Tom. "Author James Dashner's Newest:
'The Kill Order.'" *On and Beyond*, August 8, 2012.
Retrieved January 20, 2013 (http://onandbeyond
.wordpress.com/2012/08/08/author-james
-dashners-newest-the-kill-order).

It's All About Books. "Review: The Hunt for Dark Infinity
(*The 13th Reality*, Book 2) by James Dashner."
February 18, 2009. Retrieved January 20, 2013
(http://sueysbooks.blogspot.com/2009/02/
review-hunt-for-dark-infinity-by-james.html).

KalebNation.com. "Interview with James Dashner."
February 29, 2008. Retrieved December 15, 2012
(http://www.kalebnation.com/blog/2008/02/29/
interview-with-james-dashner).

Kloer, Phil. "A Fantasy About Reality." *Atlanta Journal-
Constitution*, March 6, 2008. Retrieved December
29, 2012 (http://alt.coxnewsweb.com/blogs/
content/shared-blogs/accessatlanta/atlarts/
entries/2008/03/06/a_fantasy_about_reality.html).

Lateiner Gang Book Review Spot. "Author
Interview—James Dashner." October 11, 2010.
Retrieved December 10, 2012 (http://
thelateinergangbookreviewspot.blogspot
.com/2010/10/author-interview-james-dashner
-scorch.html).

Lodge, Sally. "'*The Maze Runner*' Off to a Strong Start."
Publishers Weekly, October 22, 2009. Retrieved

December 29, 2012 (http://www.publishersweekly
.com/pw/by-topic/childrens/childrens-book-news/
article/10625-the-maze-runner-off-to-a-strong
-start.html).

Martin, Molly. "A Review of 'A Gift of Ice' by James
Dashner." Compulsive Reader, 2013. Retrieved
January 15, 2013 (http://www.compulsivereader.com
/html/index.php?name=News&file=article&sid=754).

Maw, Natasha. "Interview with James Dashner." *Maw
Books*, October 1, 2008. Retrieved January 10,
2013 (http://blog.mawbooks.com/2008/10/01/
interview-with-james-dashner-author-of-the-13th
-reality-a-journal-of-curious-letters).

Our Time in Juvie. "Author Spotlight: Interview with James
Dashner, Part 1." January 30, 2012. Retrieved
January 24, 2013 (http://www.ourtimeinjuvie.com/
author-spotlight/author-spotlight-interview-with
-james-dashner-part-i).

Our Time in Juvie. "Author Spotlight: Interview with James
Dashner, Part 2." January 30, 2012. Retrieved
January 24, 2013 (http://www.ourtimeinjuvie.com/
author-spotlight/author-spotlight-interview-with
-james-dashner-part-ii).

Pavao, Kate. "Q&A with James Dashner." *Publishers
Weekly*, August 2, 2012. Retrieved January 11,
2013 (http://www.publishersweekly.com/pw/by-
topic/authors/interviews/article/53380-q-a-with
-james-dashner.html).

Pinkston, Tristi. "Author Interview—James Dashner."
Families.com, November 6, 2006. Retrieved

December 10, 2012 (http://www.families.com/
blog/author-interview-james-dashner).

RandomBuzzers.com. "Dashner Download #1!"
February 27, 2013. Retrieved March 13, 2013
(http://www.randombuzzers.com/blog/view/
the-buzz/dashner-download-1/2013/02/27).

Riordan, Rick. "Save the Date: 'Infinity Ring,' by
James Dashner." New York Times, August 23,
2012. Retrieved December 12 (http://www
.nytimes.com/2012/08/26/books/review/infinity
-ring-by-james-dashner.html?_r=0).

Rojek, Ross. "James Dashner." Audible Authors,
October 10, 2009. Retrieved December 10,
2012 (http://audibleauthors.net/james-dashner).

Sambuchino, Chuck. "7 Things I've Learned So Far,
by James Dashner." Writer's Digest, March 23,
2010. Retrieved January 5, 2013 (http://www
.writersdigest.com/editor-blogs/guide-to
-literary-agents/7-things-ive-learned-so-far-by
-james-dashner).

Schulze, Bianca. "Bestselling Author James Dashner
on 'The Maze Runner' Trilogy & Prequel."
Children's Book Review, August 22, 2012.
Retrieved December 10, 2012 (http://www
.thechildrensbookreview.com/weblog/2012/08/
bestselling-author-james-dashner-on-the-maze
-runner-trilogy-prequel.html).

Shill, Aaron. "Accountant to Author: James Dashner
Trumps the Odds." Deseret News, July 1, 2009.
Retrieved December 10, 2012 (http://www

.deseretnews.com/article/705314078/
Accountant-to-author-James-Dashner-trumps
-the-odds.html?pg=all).

Stettler, Jeremiah. "Quitting His Day Job." *Salt Lake City Tribune*, March 6, 2008. Retrieved December 20, 2012 (http://www.sltrib.com/valleywest/ci_8477104).

Stone, Eric James. "Writer Interview: James Dashner." EricJamesStone.com, September 19, 2006. Retrieved December 14, 2012 (http://www.ericjamesstone.com/blog/2006/09/19/writer-interview-james-dashner).

Su, Steph. "Interview with James Dashner!" *Steph Su Reads*, December 14, 2009. Retrieved December 11, 2012 (http://stephsureads.blogspot.com/2009/12/interview-with-james-dashner.html).

Vice, Jeff. "James Dashner Hits It Big with Series." *Deseret News*, April 23, 2010. Retrieved December 2, 2012 (http://www.deseretnews.com/article/705377839/James-Dashner-hits-it-big-with-series.html?pg=all).

Ward, Marsha. "Author Interview: James Dashner." *Writer in the Pines*, March 5, 2008. Retrieved December 14, 2012 (http://marshaward.blogspot.com/2008/03/author-interview-james-dashner.html).

Wildner, Kristine. "James Dashner and The Maze Runner Trilogy." Curled Up with a Good Kid's Book, 2012. Retrieved December 29, 2012 (http://www.curledupkids.com/intervue/interview_james_dashner.html).

Wright, Sarah Ressler. "Author Interview: James Dashner." *Vocab Gal*, October 18, 2012. Retrieved December

12, 2012 (http://info.sadlier.com/Vocabulary-Blog/
bid/88102/Author-Interview-James-Dashner).

YA Highway. "Interview with James Dashner." March 22,
2010. Retrieved December 29, 2012 (http://www
.yahighway.com/2010/03/interview-with-james
-dashner.html).

Yin, Maryann. "James Dashner Inks 3-Book Deal at
Random House Children's Books." Mediabistro
.com, September 21, 2012. Retrieved March 13,
2013 (http://www.mediabistro.com/galleycat/
james-dashner-inks-3-book-deal-at-random
-house-childrens-books_b57902).

INDEX

ABOUT THE AUTHOR

Philip Wolny is a writer and editor from Queens, New York, and a fan of fantasy and science fiction since his early childhood.

PHOTO CREDITS

Cover, p. 3 Maria Woods; pp. 6-7 Ken Karp; p. 11 David Livingston/Getty Images; p. 12 E. Charbonneau/ WireImage/Getty Images; p. 14 © Globe Photos/ ZUMA Press; pp. 16–17 iStockphoto/Thinkstock; p. 20 George Frey/Getty Images; pp. 27, 62–63, 74–75 © AP Images; p. 31 Manuel Nauta/Landov; p. 36 Donald Uhrbrock/Time & Life Pictures/Getty Images; p. 39 Mitchell Reichler; p. 41 Ingram Publishing/ Thinkstock; p. 45 Philip Toscano/Press Association/ AP Images; p. 47 Kathleen Dusseault; p. 53 Marc Andrew Deley/Getty Images; pp. 54–55 Hiroyuki Ito/Hulton Archive/Getty Images; p. 66 The King's English Bookshop; pp. 72–73 PRNewsFoto/Scholastic Corporation/AP Images; p. 77 Hemera/Thinkstock; cover and interior pages background (marbleized texture) javarman/Shutterstock.com; cover and interior pages (book) www.iStockphoto.com/Andrzej Tokarski; interior pages background (seascape) djgis/ Shutterstock.com.

Designer: Nicole Russo; Editor: Kathy Kuhtz Campbell; Photo Researcher: Amy Feinberg